Copyright © 2019 Magic Walls & Canvas. All rights reserved.

ISBN: 978-0-6484235-1-5

All rights reserved. No part of this publication may be reproduced or transmitted in any form or by any means, electronic or mechanical, including photocopying, recording, storage in an information retrieval system, or otherwise, without the prior written permission of the publisher, unless specifically permitted under the Australian Copyright ACT 1968 as amended.

Written by Anissa Papadakos
Illustrated by Anissa Papadakos
Text copyright © Anissa Papadakos
Illustration copyright © Anissa Papadakos

Visit: www.magicwallsandcanvas.com

Facebook: Anissa Papadakos
Magic Walls & Canvas
Instagram: magicwallsandcanvas

NATIONAL LIBRARY OF AUSTRALIA

A catalogue record for this book is available from the National Library of Australia

To all mothers out there
(young & old or soon to be)

You're all a Wonder Woman

Special Thanks to my Husband & Family

Dear Wonder Woman

Thank you for purchasing "The Brochure Lied". I hope it brightens your day and assures you that you're an amazing mother who is doing an amazing job.

When I became a first time mum I lost myself, I lost my identity. I didn't know who I was and what I was doing.

I struggled emotionally and I struggled physically, and at the time not fully understanding my situation, I sought help from the wrong people. People who couldn't support me and people who couldn't hear me when I asked for help.

There were many mothers who never mentioned anything about feeling lost, of being unsure or anxious, of feeling sad or depressed. Nobody ever talked about not enjoying motherhood, difficulty with breastfeeding or not feeling connected with their baby.

I didn't understand why I was the only one experiencing these things and that's why I struggled for nearly 2.5 years.

Now that I am expecting my second child, all these emotions are slowly creeping back. The difference this time is I have a better understanding of how to deal with these emotions. Throughout this journey I have also realised that even professionals can get it wrong - you will be very surprised where the right answers truly come from.

Now, I know who to speak to if I need advice and most of all I know that what I am feeling is normal, that I am beautiful and not a mess.

I hope this book empowers you, empowers all women to support each other by speaking up and discussing these feelings which today still affects us all. If we stand together, support each other and speak up we are not only leading the way for our children but we are bringing true power to ourselves.

xoxo

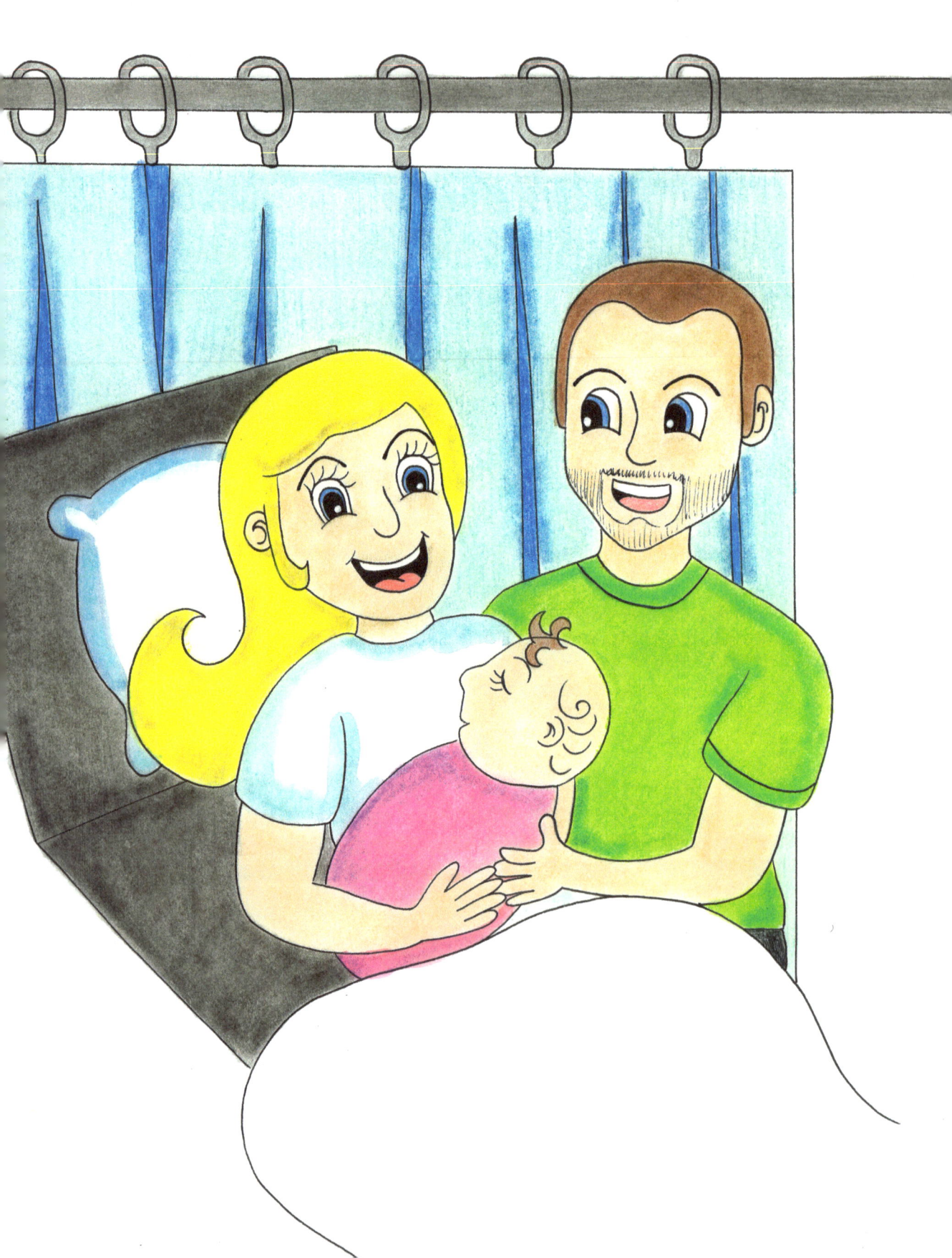

What a beautiful moment it was

The moment we first laid our eyes on you; our baby

The doctors and nurses showed you to us; you looked so cute, like a roly poly puppy dog

You screamed so loud

We cried with joy

Your daddy cut your umbilical cord and dressed you up from head to toe

And then finally, I got the chance to hold you

I could not believe it

I had just become a mother!

My emotions were flying and I felt like a mess

I honestly didn't know what to feel deep down and couldn't settle to get some much-needed rest

Before I knew it the visitors had arrived

They brought lots of flowers and toys and gave kisses, hugs and high fives

"Ohh Ahh the baby is beautiful", they said. "How precious, how sacred; you are incredibly blessed"

REASSURANCE

If only I could go back to that moment

The moment when I first met you and started feeling like a mess

I would reassure myself that what I was feeling is -

1. normal and not abnormal
2. that I am beautiful, and
3. certainly not a mess

But if this reassurance does not help, I would tell myself to please speak up

Confide in someone honest and genuine, who will help and guide you out of the emotional mess

When all the visitors had left and the laughter and the cheers had subsided

All who remained in our ward was just me, your dad and you sleeping in your bassinet beside us

We watched you as you laid there

To us it felt like hours

It was just too surreal to believe that we had become parents

Then out of nowhere you started to stir and cry

So I popped my left boob out but you said "No thanks mum, not the right beverage for tonight"

That's when I realised the <u>brochure had lied</u>!

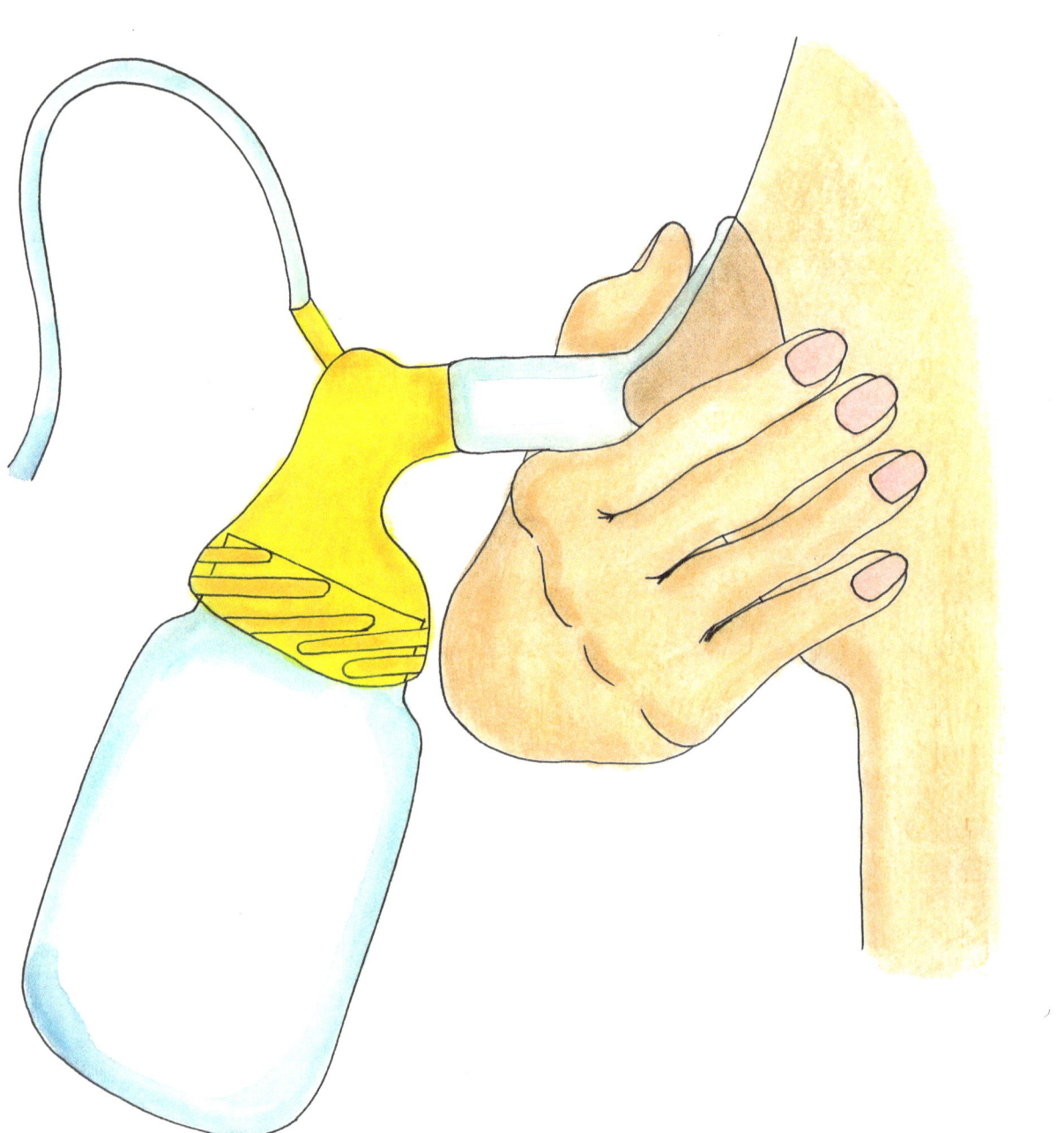

The first night was hard

It was so hard for me

Neither boob wanted to work to feed my baby

We tried everything

We gave them a massage, we tried to squeeze and even gave them a good old fashioned tug

Then finally, after baby's constant screaming we decided to try the breast pump

But as I sat there pumping my boobs, I just couldn't believe what I had gone through

In my mind I remember the brochure said this was going to be easy and then it dawned on me.......

My God, that same brochure had lied to me

By the time we reached the morning, I was numb and tired

My hair was a birds nest and my emotions were fried

I didn't get much sleep

Sleep is what I desperately need

I need to close my eyes and rest

Just five more minutes please

But that five minutes never came

Not at all

It was just me in the room listening to you cry some more

There was nothing else to do but to pick you up and hold you tight

I just didn't quite understand why my new role, I absolutely despised

Then it suddenly dawned on me, the brochure had lied

The brochure said that I would be happy

It said that I would be overjoyed and giddy

But all I felt like was a broken dairy cow with an udder which did not work as described

I felt sad

I felt tired and worn out and all I wanted to do was cry

Why did the brochure have to lie?

REASSURANCE

If only I could go back to that moment

The moment when my breasts could not function at their best

I would reassure myself that what I was feeling is -

1. normal and not abnormal
2. that I am beautiful, and
3. certainly not a mess

I would reassure myself that breast feeding is hard

It is not something which happens without a hitch

And if Bub doesn't want to latch onto your boob, be gentle on yourself and not a judgemental witch

But if this reassurance does not help, I would tell myself to please speak up and seek help

Even Daddy was beginning to break

He looked tired from worry and was starting to lose weight

He walked into our room with bags under his eyes

He wasn't clean shaven, oh my what a surprise

There was no hug and no kiss first thing for me but he took one deep breath and uttered ever so quietly:

"I don't think we thought this through"

I froze in my spot after he uttered those seven words; surely I must have misheard

But the expression on his face said it all, so I looked him dead in the eyes and replied, "Mmm it's a bit too late for you to make that call"

Calendar

				1	2 Check List - Bottles - Dummies - Nappies - Bumb rash cream	3
				12 days to go...		
4	5 Note To Self - Never do this again!	6 Pram is READY! YAY	7	8 My back hurts. Need more pillows at night.	9	10 Plenty of bottles, just in case my boobs don't work!
11 Feel heavy today- too much ice cream.	12 Bag is Packed. Excited Today!	13 Hospital Check In! (Getting nervous)	14 Meet Baby	15 Day 1. Dont feel good. Why?	16 Day 2. Oh My God! - My boobs dont work - I am beyond tired...	17 Day 3. What is going on?
18 Day 4. Not Happy Jan!!! :(	19 Day 5. What go home? They must be joking!	20	21	22	23	24
25	26 - My boobs dont work - this cant be happening	27 HOME TIME - NO - Not Ready, no siree	28	29 happy to stay longer	30 Just a couple more days I promise I will be good :)	

Before we knew it, the Hospital said it was time to pack up and go home

I felt even more lost, confused and alone

My baby did not want to latch onto my boobs

My baby did not even want to nap or snooze

The only thing that baby wanted to do was to cry to the point where even I turned blue

And for these reasons alone is why I was not happy with the idea of going home

I just didn't understand why the brochure said that it would be a happy moment; one which I would never forget

Happy is not the word I would use and it is best to not repeat the word I did use

However, it was certainly a moment which I cannot forget

It was the moment that made me very upset

As I looked at the suitcases beside my bed; putting it simply, the brochure had lied yet again

We loaded the car

Daddy made sure baby was strapped in

I sat next to Bub not excited, but numb, scared and drawn within

Today, years later, I understand why I was in such a gloom

I was simply tired and anxious

And a new mum who had no clue

I just wished someone, anyone in that moment was true

Not fake and misleading or a Pinocchio mind you

I just needed some reassurance and a little genuine advice

That the journey ahead was going to be <u>hard</u> but <u>nice</u>

But at that moment while I sat in the car full of despair

Nothing, absolutely nothing, could change my mind, the marvellous brochure had lied

REASSURANCE

If only I could go back to that moment

That moment on my way home when I felt like a mess

I would reassure myself that what I was feeling is -

1. normal and not abnormal
2. that I am beautiful, and
3. certainly not a mess

I would tell myself while I sat in the car that I am beyond capable by far

I would tell myself that I can do this, for certain I can

I am already doing a great job, stop worrying girlfriend

But if this reassurance does not help, I would tell myself to please seek help

Confide in someone honest and true who will help and guide you through

Back to that Wonder Woman, who is still inside of you

We finally arrive home

Daddy drove slow, as slow as a snail can be

We unloaded the car and stepped into the house

We looked at each other and said "What now?"

Mummy puts sleeping baby into the pram and decides it's best to just lie down

To be honest, I didn't know what else to do

It was just too hard at home with you

That's why putting my head down was all I could do

As I lay there I wondered where was the joy; where was the excitement

I felt none of that except anxiety and was beginning to feel very frightened

The deeper in thought I continued to be, the only thing which made sense was that the brochure had lied to me

I remember the first night at home like it was yesterday

We placed Baby in the cot and both collapsed onto the hay

Yes I thought, finally my own pillow, my own bed

"Ah Ah AHHH", said Bub, you both will never sleep again

Bub made so many noises even though it didn't toss and turn

It made gurgling noises which made me worried and full of concern

Why were they so noisy when they slept in their bed?

Is Baby sick or am I missing it yet again?

I just don't understand how this can be

The brochure sure did not say anything to me

Was this in the fine print which I didn't read?

But as I lay there staring at the ceiling, I just could not shake the bad feeling

That the brochure which I had been reading was utterly misleading

After about my tenth coffee the next morning, I still felt dishevelled and like a zombie

So I sat there deep in thought, trying to make sense my feeling of distraught

Yes, I know I love my baby yes I do

Even though there was no connection between us that felt good and true

Wait a minute was that the clue?

But before I could ponder even more there was a knock on the door

And with no warning, no warning at all, visitors marched through the door which did not make me happy at all

Why couldn't they call and ask if it was okay?

Instead they all just came over without delay

The visitors filed in, they marched through the door all wearing a big grin

I understand why they were all excited

But I was feeling miserable and beyond tired

All I yearned for was some peace and quiet

But peace was not at hand and without warning comments began

1. "Stop mopping"
2. "You are not doing it right"
3. "How can you be tired, you should be happy and beyond delight"

But before the day was through, a bomb was dropped on you know who

The comment sent shock waves right through my body

It nearly destroyed that little amount of hope inside of me

"What did you think motherhood was going to be?"

Oh my, then it dawned on me, the brochure had lied to me

REASSURANCE

If only I could go back to that moment

That moment when I felt exhausted and a complete mess

I would reassure myself that what I was feeling is -

1. normal
2. I am beautiful, and
3. not a mess.

I would tell myself that everybody has a way of doing things right

It may not be clear but if it works for you stick to it my dear

And please keep in mind that you may not be happy, bubbly and bright

That's okay because who could have known what motherhood would really be like

But if none of this reassurance helps, please go and seek genuine help

It is not just you Wonder Woman who is struggling with this

It is every other mother who is tired and new to this

There are plenty of great things about being a mum

They are just tarnished by lack of sleep, stress, anxiety and fear

But when that difficult moment comes about

I want you to promise me one thing

That you will stop, take a deep breath and seek help

While help is on its way, please look back and remember the special moments of each day:

1. Your Baby's first smile
2. Your Baby's first giggle
3. Cuddles you share
4. Bath time
5. Singing to Baby
6. Seeing your baby happy and smiling

FINAL WORDS

If none of my words have helped, absolutely none at all

Please understand that it's not just you going through this all

It's every mother big and small

We all think we are crazy and we all think we are wrong

Let me reassure you, you have simply been tired all along

If you need help, just reach out without despair

There are plenty of amazing people out there

They will guide you and support you while you are feeling down

But always remember to take a moment

A moment to breath

You're doing an amazing job

You'll get there, you'll see

Know that help is always at hand, talking about it gives you Power Girlfriend

Here are their details, so just reach out.......

PANDA
1300 726 306
www.panda.org.au
Supports families affected by anxiety and depression

Lifeline
If you, or someone you know, are experiencing emotional distress, please call Lifeline 13 11 14 (24 hours/7 days) or chat to a crises supporter on-line at lifeline.org.au (7pm-midnight/7 nights)
If life is in danger, please call 000

Beyond Blue
1300 22 4363
www.beyondblue.org.au
Provide information and support to help everyone to achieve their best mental health

National Breastfeeding Helpline
1800 686 268
www.pregnancybirthbaby.org.au
Provides advice and support on breastfeeding

Pregnancy, Birth and Baby
1800 882 436
www.pregnancybirthbaby.org.au
Provides advice and support for parents and families

Healthdirect
1800 022 222
www.healthdirect.gov.au
Provides 24 hour advice and information

Red Nose
1300 308 307
www.rednose.com.au
Provide advice and information on safe sleeping for baby

Emergency
000
If you or someone else is seriously injured or in need of urgent medical help, call triple zero immediately

www.ingramcontent.com/pod-product-compliance
Lightning Source LLC
Chambersburg PA
CBHW042141290426
44110CB00002B/78